RELATIONSHIP

RECOVERY

BY

ANTHONY BROWN

Table of Contents

INTRODUCTION

I was sitting with a female client and she was sharing about her relationship. She described it as unfulfilling. I could see she was on her way to transitioning out of it. She was afraid of the prospect of being alone and starting all over again. Women don't like to start over, they are all about maintaining. Maintaining a relationship in a static state of happiness and contentment is impossible. Relationships are constantly evolving and changing as both parties root themselves more and more into each other's lives and destinies. Female clients often ask me advice on how to maintain their balance and interest in an uninteresting relationship scenario. I can't inject excitement into a boring movie's plot. I would just assume walk out of the theatre and try and forget the experience altogether. The issue is I'm a guy and women aren't wired that way. They have a relationship salvage mechanism that can't be bypassed. I told my client that she needed to work on herself because she couldn't work on him. That was his job to do. I told her to amplify her sense of value, beauty, inner strength and awareness through positive affirmation. I knew I would hear from her again. I knew when I did she would be in tears from the start, or at some point during the conversation because the relationship she asked me to help her save had dissolved.

My concern is always my client's wellbeing and sense of joy, not her partner's choice. I can't control that. I am writing this book for women. At some point every woman will face the reality that relationships end. The time in between a relationship ending and a woman being available for new love to blossom in her life is called recovery. I am going to help you understand that there is a cycle, broken into phases, that is natural and necessary to facilitate this healing. I call it The Relationship Recovery Cycle.

I am an intuitive coach that specializes in dating and relationship, health and wellness, and diet and exercise. My background is in the area of ministry. I also spent almost 8 years as a United States Marine. Although I have helped many clients in the areas of expertise I ascribe to as a coach, it must be understood from the start that my advice is based on an intuitive gift I have operated in all my life. It arises from my spiritual intuition and instinct, not a college degree or any documented clinical experience. The principles I teach I have lived and experienced first-hand. I have watched many lives change for the better and been very touched and blessed to help people become more self-aware. I can help any woman who needs relationship wisdom and clarity through this and other forthcoming books I will write as well as one on one coaching, and workshops that specifically amplify the philosophies I teach. I respect any skepticism received and welcome all resistance, retreat and denial. I love every human being on the face of this earth, every life form that expresses its presence I adore, every breath I get to take is one that I thank the universe for, and I am always learning and evolving more into me. If you read this book with an open mind, your life will benefit from it. I wrote this book for women because I know you are a precious gift to the universe and a powerful force in raising mankind to a new level of consciousness.

The Relationship Recovery Cycle is composed of four phases; **Sadness**, **Anger**, **Confusion**, and **Joy**. This cycle is not for recovery from one-night stands or calls of the booty. It also doesn't apply to physically abusive relationships (Chapter 5 covers the protocol for these instances specifically), or relationships that have lasted less than 6 months in general with few exceptions (Chapters 6 & 7 cover a few of these). It takes time to develop a true bond with another human being. Only you, as a woman, will know whether or not a short term relationship of six months or less impacted your heart and soul to the point of needing this process of healing. Here is a general rule…If you grew to deeply care for him, understanding this recovery cycle and its phases will facilitate you bouncing back much faster. If you didn't grow to care for your ex deeply to the point of strong attachment, then date others until the hold of your infatuation for him leaves and the draw of his influence fades.

I look at my mother. I see years of pain from loving men in the past that never loved her back in a way that sustained or fulfilled. She now has the love that she has always dreamt of. I want all women to experience this…it requires relationship recovery.

Anthony Brown - 2016

CHAPTER 1

SADNESS

IT'S OVER AND I CAN'T STOP CRYING

Women have the capacity to cry. Cry like life as they know it is
ending. Mucus volcano, waterfall simulations of river madness!
There's no abating the flow or understanding the waterlogged, vocal-
chord disabled jargon. To say the word "he" is impossible. It
chokes out so much and so many times that the context after it has
no meaning. I'll finish the statement so we can move on and start
the healing process. The statement is "He broke up with me"

The sadness you feel hurts your body like a plumber's wrench to
the gut. Why wear makeup? Fuck makeup! Bathing is going to be
optional for weeks, not a mandatory task at all. No razor, wax,
lipstick, or attractive clothing will touch your emotionally bruised
and battered body at this time. You're wearing a potato sack and
eating ice cream that contains 1500 calories per scoop.

This is ground zero. Don't call your girlfriends yet, they'll just tell you to hydrate because there's no helping you in this state. Don't call any guy friends because this is the only state in which you'd take a guy out of the friend zone to fuck him. He knows this and absolutely won't let you get decently dressed. His goal is to get you out of your pajamas so you can really relax, feel me? Sadness has no reason or root, it just hurts. I'll end this thought with the bad news first. It hurts more than you can fathom.

The good news comes now. The sadness you feel is necessary and natural. It has to run its course and the best state to be in while dealing with it is alone. Your desire to be alone and under a comfy blanket is normal and healthy. Don't let your girlfriends come over at this time. You don't want their company right now anyway. Your instincts are right and your desire to smell like a hairy skunk-rat is not going to be appreciated by your girlfriends. Society tells you to surround yourself with support but if you do, friendships will be damaged, I guarantee.

You're going to be tired, really tired. Work is going to feel like hell on earth and every request will be impossible. Allow sadness to run its course, don't fight it or try to work over or through it. If you surrender to its process it will only take a few days to get to the end of this initial crisis feeling. If you resist, try and stop the tears or put on a happy face then you will take forever to leave this initial waterpark reaction. It will come out in seizure-like attacks that will be triggered by the strangest things. If you try and tough it out and be a modern woman about it you will damage yourself emotionally and it will be hard to come back from that, trust me.

After three days this initial meltdown will be done. Why three days? It took 3 days for Christ to rise from the dead. You feel dead right now don't you? Take three days, and if it takes more than we can talk about the legal ramifications of my statement. Humor is your greatest weapon as a woman to fight off and equalize the bitterness that will come. Give it three days. Women experience a relationship death and it's real for them. Three days are a reference point for you to consciously not attack, judge, or condemn yourself to a psychiatric facility before that timeframe has elapsed. You can make it.

The next part of sadness especially hurts men. The bottom line…you hate dick. Sex is the physical exchange between a man and a woman that differentiates friendship from intimacy. You were intimate with this dude and he broke your heart. If he hadn't had sex with you then you wouldn't be feeling this way. You still miss his smile, his laugh and his presence. His dick is now the enemy because you still want it, but can't have it. So all dicks are the enemy because you can't have the one you want. My advice to guys during this time would be to stay clear of you. Women say the most hurtful things during this period because all men are scum at this time, because they have dicks. A woman wants one dick at this time, her ex's. The problem is that she wants to smash it to a pulp just as much receive it like the savior it is. I wrote this book for women so my advice to any woman at this time would be to stay clear of men and do no mental or physical harm if she has to interact with them.

The hate dick part of this phase can last for weeks, yes weeks. It can last for months but that is usually due to a woman breaking the recovery cycle by going from sadness into a pleasure rejection mode. This is the woman who says she hasn't had sex for a year by choice and acts like she's proud of it. She's not proud. She's decided to be a cold hearted bitch and totally close herself off from passionate connection with a loving man. If you are making this decision for religious reason my comment doesn't apply to you. If you have a medical condition that affects your sexual desire level than I'm not talking to you. If you're just a sexual deviant that lives by the beat of your own weird drum this doesn't apply to you. The context is you have ended a relationship, are overcome with sadness, and instead of moving to the anger phase of the recovery cycle, decide not to cycle anymore at all. You then back out of physical relationship exchange because you are afraid of getting hurt again. My advice is to let the phase naturally express itself to its end. You'll be happier in the long run if you do.

The last part of this phase is depression. "The world sucks right now" will be your general consensus about life at this time. Women love knowing, feeling, and experiencing the tangible presence of their partner. When a relationship ends that loss of presence is devastating. Nothing you do has meaning because your man's presence brings meaning and fullness to your experience. You will feel like life is empty at this time. This is necessary. It's necessary to feel this way so when you wake up and realize that no human being deserves that much power in your life, the truth of that revelation will stick. If you deny the weight of the emotions behind the ridiculous notions you feel then you do yourself a disservice. Most coaches would encourage you to affirm a more positive outlook at this time. I disagree with that sentiment. You and your partner were one organism and now that organism is dead and you are alone to fend for and nourish yourself individually. The hole that was caused from the break up must close and heal so you can be complete again. A woman has to separate herself as an entity from the entity that was the relationship. Once she does this she's ready to move from sadness to the next phase of the recovery cycle. The transition time is related to who you are, how deeply you loved, and how much you lost yourself in your partner's energy and identity. My advice is to let it be as long as it needs to be. You'll feel the shift take place because one morning you will wake up and simply say, "What the fuck am I doing, I need to shower this man's bullshit off of my sexy body!"

A note before we move on to the next chapter. I could never teach or instruct a woman on how to be a woman. My specialty is relationship dynamics. We are talking about how a woman can properly cycle out of an ended relationship with a man and recover her spiritual, mental and physical identity. She can then be available fully for a new, fulfilling relationship to enter her life. I don't know if the Relationship Recovery Cycle works the same for lesbians, gays, or any other relationship dynamic. Maybe it does, I just don't know because my spiritual intuition and instinct on this subject are predicated upon characteristics I find inherently present in men and women and how those qualities interact in that relationship context. If you are lesbian and the principles work for you awesome, if gay and they work, great. Masculine and feminine dynamics tend to govern behavior in similar ways no matter what gender of skin they reside in so I wouldn't be surprised.

If you really want to cry…cry

Hydrate the barrenness of your heart's pain with the love of your

soul's caress

Anthony Brown-2015

CHAPTER 2

ANGER

FUCK HIM AND HIS NEW BITCH!

When we wake up from the sadness of what was we realize the anger of what is. Anger in the beginning comes from a place of helplessness, not empowerment. It's the feeling you have after you've been robbed of something that can't be recovered. It's the feeling that your life has more value than the time you just wasted. Anger is simple. You look at your life and simply say "Fuck that" which turns into "Fuck him" which finally ends up at "Fuck everything". This is necessary and healthy. I'm going to be the one man who tells every woman reading this text that the crazy fluctuations in anger that you feel after a break up are not only necessary, but beneficial. Sadness is like a blanket of syrup that covers your body and makes you stick to everything you don't want to hold onto. Anger is a firehose directed straight at you that says, "Get your sticky ass out of bed, this motherfucker's not worth it." Anger is always directed at others, only after it washes you first. In the end anger is the catalyst for empowered change and detachment from the failed relationship, but you're not there yet.

Now let's hit the best catalyst for anger head on. Why play and ruin my rep by beating around the new bush? Yes, the new bush has already arrived and you're furious about it. The new woman. It's only been three weeks and this juggernaut level asshole has a new woman. Anger from deep within starts to surface. You're connecting your value level with the amount of time it took for him to bounce back. Ladies let me set you free about something.

It's not about you...

Johnny looks in his black book. His ex-girlfriend deleted all his contacts out of his cell phone in anger after she found the "P" pics in his phone. He's dusting off years of pain and pleasure on each weathered page and he lands on Gina's name. He remembers and smiles. "Damn she was nice, a real giver." He thinks about the good times and they outweigh the crazy ones. The crazy ones were kind of fun too, although at the time he was thinking about getting a restraining order. Tammy, his ex, rushes back into his thoughts.

She's just too much to forget. Too loving, too forgiving, too crazy in the right way. She had a right to throw his shit out the window, from the second floor. The sprinklers were going but, damn, coming face to face with another woman's jungle pussy on an I-phone can do that to a woman. "I love this woman. I gotta work this out!" 15 texts later, 5 phone calls with messages left, and 7 pics from past good times sent. Still no response. He's out of his mind now. This is too important to give up on. If he could just talk to her in person than they could work things out. He goes to her job. He texts her and requests she come out so they can talk. She texts back saying she never wants to see him again. All Tammy sees when she envisions Bryan in her mind is a dude with some skank bitch's pussy resting on top of his body instead of a head. She's disgusted by that. Bryan is desperate. He has to talk to her. Just then, an ugly dude in a suit comes by and says, "You have to move your car, you're parked in my space." Bryan ignores him at first then tells Tammy's department manager to back off for a minute. He's irritated and his anger is escalating. He then looks at George more closely. That's the dude that was hitting on Tammy at last year's Christmas party. Man he wanted to kick that dude's ass but he held back because she begged him to. Now this

fucktard wanted his parking space.

Ladies, I don't want to turn this into a Lifetime network tragedy

but you know what comes next. Bryan gets into a physical

altercation with George. George kicks Bryan's ass. Bryan gets his

gun from the trunk of his car and shoots George. He finds Tammy

in her cubicle. He just wants Tammy back. She isn't speaking to

this pussy-headed maniac. He takes the gun out and puts it to his

head. He says, "Talk to me or I'll blow my fuckin brains out!"

I know you want to know the ending. Let's just skip it because
women have many versions of it and they're all bad. My advice is to
be thankful for Gina. Be angry but thankful.

I wrote this book for women because men don't cycle, they just
move forward. They don't have the emotional capacity or
complexity to do so. It's a gift for women, not a tragedy, when men
move forward quickly and get on with their lives. It allows a woman
to process her feelings in peace, without fear or insecurity. There's
my long version of saying it's not about you.

Anger comes from not knowing what he is doing, not feeling his presence abiding over you. He left his real job, fuck UPS. His real job was taking care of you and he quit like a little bitch! All the things you did to make his life better, all the ways you changed for him so he would be happy. Women can't believe it when men leave, they just can't wrap their minds around how a man could leave perfection for the gutter experience of someone new. Anger is irrational and causes you to have all these sentiments and the amplified feelings that go along with them. Anger isn't just rage, it has more range than that. It's how we express our frustration and discontentment when we have no appropriate filter for it. It's the rawness of our emotion's pain expressed through the irritation of reality's current situation. It's necessary for a woman to take all this to its end…clarity. Clarity comes when you realize that you're done. Regardless of how you feel, you are done. Despite the pain you feel, further engagement in hope is futile. Now it's time to be bolstered and built back up by your friends, girlfriends specifically.

"He was never good enough for you." "He's a loser." "You're so hot and he's so not." "I never liked him, just dealt with his tired ass for your sake." Women have a hard time admitting how much better they feel when they hear these types of statements. Your girlfriends have one job during the anger phase. That is to take your ex-boyfriend off of the pedestal you built for him. Like demolishing a kitchen before the remodel. Their job is to let you know how ugly the old kitchen cabinets were. How they didn't want to cook in your kitchen before because the old range top was a disgusting grease magnet and the electric burners scared them. It's all said and amplified to give you a sense of renewed value and destroy your collective identity you shared with your ex. It's time to be and live in just you again and they are going to lead you to that self-love space by any means necessary. This is why a woman feels most betrayed when a girlfriend that does this fucks her ex. It's one of the older subliminal rules women share in friendship…ex-boyfriends are off the table. It comes off as conniving and manipulative when this trust is broken, as it should. Good friends do the dirty work so an angry woman can come out clean and empowered.

Anger lasts until clarity comes. Every woman gets to a point where she realizes there's no value in being angry anymore. What's done is done. Why is a man writing this book you might ask? Why is a man asserting things that women know naturally, even instinctively? For the same reason a guy isn't cute unless at least 3 women say he is. Women believe what men say and men believe what women say. If men say women are crazy then honestly, women tend to adopt that sentiment. If a sexy woman saw a man in her office wearing a pink plaid shirt and came over to him and said, "That shirt is so sexy on you," then handed him her wet panties…he would wear that pink plaid shirt every day. That would become his lucky shirt. Every dude from twenty feet or closer would say, "Change that shirt bro, it's a crime!" As long as the sexy woman he wants comes by and smiles when he wears it, he'll keep wearing it. I'm saying this once and for all, women aren't crazy. They're are just women. Men are not crazy, they're just men.

A man sees a woman eating a hotdog and she looks at him and smiles while taking another bite…That's the definition of love at first site

The same woman turns to her left and kisses her dog's wet mouth,

with tongue, and then looks back at the man and smiles again...this

woman is angry, avoid this woman at all costs

Anthony Brown-2015

CHAPTER 3

CONFUSION

I'M GOING TO FIGURE THIS OUT, EVEN IF IT KILLS ME!

As I'm writing this I'm possessed by purpose. I have pressure coming at me from all sides. Life has taken the only turn it ever has for me. A turn for the best during the worst circumstances. The movie in the background reflects this. The pain in my heart still resonates with every keystroke. The reality that no matter how much I channel, how deeply I love, how far I have come in life…the electric bill is still overdue. I'm confused. I thought being in the flow of love brought freedom, not oppression. I thought exercising my faith over and over again would bring hope, not despair. I'm not depressed, not happy or unhappy, and certainly not wealthy. I don't even want money. I want the cycle of my life's adventure to stop for a moment so I can understand it better. I want the noise of the pain in my shoulder to cease its ringing. I want to understand enough in each moment. I just want clarity that lies beyond the end of each purpose's narrative. I'm confused about everything and nothing at the same time. I know why I was put on this earth finally, but why does my shoulder hurt?

Confusion keeps us moving forward towards clarity because only a forward direction ends in a clear path. Trying to figure out everything along the way is an intoxicating diversion into the unknown realm of why? How? Where? What now?

Women like to know why he left. The want to know what deficiency caused his mind and heart to stray from their grasp into another woman's peace. It's not possible to turn off this mechanism of mind numbing detective work from a woman's conscious drive. If I could harness this drive into my life's direction and direct its power towards my goals and dreams, I'd be richer than Steve Jobs by now. If being rich were the end game, I'd be set. That's not even the beginning of wisdom, however, so I will digress from its influence and stick to the vision at hand. My wisdom leads me to one end, enlightenment through Love's expression. I want women to be free to embrace every aspect of their collective beings, and I'm tired of that expression being stifled because mankind can't handle the manifestation of Love's nuance that so beautifully flows through their soul's song. This is my poetic way of saying it's alright to be confused after a break up. There are thousands of questions that need to be answered and each answer has its own direction and track to follow.

I got too fat. I stopped being attentive. He always planned to leave. My intelligence intimidated him. His best friend wanted me and he couldn't handle it. I was too jealous. He had a problem with my neurotic cleanliness. My personality pissed him off constantly. I was too short for him. I was too tall and made him look like an elf next to me. My pussy wasn't tight enough. His dick was curved and I never came. I didn't give him enough blowjobs. He had a problem with my job. I was always asking him when he was going to get a job. My feet are ugly. He's a boob man and I wouldn't get surgery. I didn't want to have kids. He didn't want to have kids.

These statements lead to questions that need to be answered for clarity and peace. You're very smart and have allotted time in each day to get them answered. Your girlfriends want you to get back on your horse and let these mindless pursuits go. That's the problem, they are not mindless, but mindful and have to be addressed. Any dates at this time will be hell on earth because the new guy sitting at the other end of the table becomes a test subject for these issues to get addressed. This poor sucker needs to answer the "why do guys do this?" questions. He's not equipped, trust me. Men do things based on the need to shit, eat, sleep and fuck when it comes to women. It's a primal formula that no form of complicated thinking can unravel or solve. Keep asking those questions and watch your date go into a coma.

Don't fight this phase. Dive into it until you run out of steam. Go full CSI Miami and take blood, hair and stool samples. Call your friends in law enforcement and do profile analysis. Tell your girlfriends that you think your ex was in the CIA and go about trying to prove it. I'm not joking. I'm not patronizing. The harder you attack this phase with focus, the shorter it is. You will arrive at the truth soon enough. You'll get an answer but the truth doesn't rely in any of your answers power. The truth is he's gone and you couldn't stop it. You figured out how to stop it but you can't go back in time so it's irrelevant. You finally understood why he didn't want a lap dance during the Super Bowl. It wasn't halftime, but that was 2013 and now it's 2015 and he doesn't give a shit about football anymore since his dad died. He used to watch the games with him every year. His dad was a football fanatic but now the game reminds him of his dad's lost presence so he'd rather do anything else than watch the game right now. Your lap dance is irrelevant. You won because you figured out why he wanted that super skank but then again you lost because he's marrying the bitch. Keep it up, keep digging, because you have to. Until you don't.

Confusion is necessary for you to grow as a person and learn how to communicate better at a relational level. Each quest that ends in you not finding out more about him and why he left forces you to look at yourself and the role you played in your relationships demise. Not from a "what's wrong with me" perspective but a much deeper level of introspection. You start thinking about what kind of person you are and what type of energy you put out into the universe and the energy you draw back from the same source. Admitting you don't have all the answers opens you up to learning the right questions. What kind of women am I? What type of man do I want in my life? How much is a relationship more about my security and control than a loving interaction between two loving souls? At the end of confusion lies a great revelation. We are all at best flawed, and even the smartest of us can lose track of what matters. What matters is that we are agents of Love in any and all relationships, of every kind, that come our way. Confused as to why it all ended? At the end of your emotional reason's rope? Good, now you can learn how to be an open soul verses a closed and damaged one. You're ready for joy and wonder to enter your thoughts again.

Stop rolling loaded dice…no matter from what angle you view their spin, any vantage point you see their journey or what theory you use to presume their resting place, they end at 7 every time

Anthony Brown-2015

CHAPTER 4

JOY

I'M NEVER GOING TO FORGET THE WONDERFUL TIMES

WE HAD

The Joy of the Lord is my strength. The Joy of my experience is the memory of my pains abatement. The joy of my existence is the love of another soul, loving me, caring for me, treating me to an ice cream cone in the rain. In the rain, of course in the rain. Because of love, every fucked up, stupid, impossibly inappropriate situation has meaning and a happy ending. When a woman says, "Never do that again" with a smile, she means it. As men we get angry. As men we miss the point. What's she's really saying is, "Don't do that again, because I love you so fuckin much that what you did should disgust me, but I actually accept it. That makes me feel extremely uncomfortable."

I want to reconnect women with relationship joy. The painful kind. The stomachache that is actually a love ache of acknowledgment. Remember your first love ladies? Every woman remembers because this dude could do no wrong. It's embarrassing, the things you forgave him for. He fucked your best friend…forgiven. He forgot to pick you up for the prom, he was drunk. He still managed to fuck you that same night, your first time. It wasn't even that good but you taught him to be good so no worries. The first got away with so much, but no more. How many married ladies still have pictures of a first love hidden in a box somewhere or in the protective hands of a mother's discretion? Your first represents the openness of your deepest heart, and its capacity to forgive and heal. Society's dream, that white picket fence, soon is shattered by the reality of how things really are. Reality turns you into a closed woman. A woman that doesn't jump, but crawls. A woman that doesn't reach but pulls toward self. Women are givers of power, grace, passion, knowledge, resourcefulness, peace, prosperity, and wisdom. You were not created to be closed vessels of credit card madness.

Every relationship has joy associated with it. One joyous moment can cancel out 15 moments of pain, 5 moments of treachery, even one moment of sexual indiscretion. It's time to let the joy of the relationship heal and help the mind of destructed fragments that were left in the ended relationship's wake. Think about it, dream of its power, and surrender to the joy the relationship brought and still can bring.

He stole flowers because he was broke as fuck. Then the yard's guardian, a pit-bull named Clarence, chased his stupid ass all the way to the fence of your front yard. They were just daisies. Five years later a guy buys you a dozen roses but you're not as impressed. Your ex risked his worthless life for those daisies. You're not worth his life, you know you're not. He did stupid shit like that all the time. The joy of it. The joy of it as you told your girlfriends about it. The jealousy in their eyes as they listened to you describe this idiocy. He was a protective son of a bitch. The protective part made you wet every time. Joy in the raw, pure acts of love a man displayed to you, who was clue-less otherwise. Maybe he had his shit together but no passion was present in his action. You felt the joy of knowing your security was set. He would fix anything but you. You were his perfect queen. You loved the pedestal you didn't earn. There's joy in that. I'm talking about how women really feel, not how society filters your reality. I teach men how to act so they can attract, keep and grow with the women they want. Most men are a mix of effective and ineffective qualities. Women have an enormous capacity to amplify the effectivity of man's inspired moments, his dynamism. That's what joy is all about, amplification.

The joy heals. It heals your heart and washes away bitterness. You can't be bitter and full of joy at the same time. The opposite of joy isn't hate, it is bitterness. Joy speaks of an outlook that amplifies a one-ness mindset in all circumstance and situation. Remember how good he was at making you feel good. His smell, the natural scent that agreed with your sensibility. It is one thing to smell good, but he smelled right. A lot of men try and try to be funny but he actually was. The humor smoothed out a lot of his rough edges. He hid the truth from you, he was a great cook and when he made that special dinner one night you felt so special. These actions don't keep a couple together but they make great moments. Moments full of joy. I teach my clients how to display the qualities necessary for longevity and fulfillment in a relationship. But joyous moments are just that, a refreshing time of deep breaths and endearing smiles. Let the simple, happy times wash the wounds of the biting and harsh trials experienced. It's time to be happy again. Maybe even meet a new person to share that happiness with.

I saw a women walking with a man on the wet-sand part of the beach. She looked happy and he was elated. They stopped at the perfect spot and kissed under the sun as it set. I looked at my wife and said, "How was your walk with Snapper," our boxer. She said "Any time away from you is a good time" and laughed her ass off. I laughed my ass off with her and she then said, "Any time with you is that much better baby"

Just then I heard a man exclaim from behind the lovebirds on the beach, "Cut, that's a wrap"

Anthony Brown-2015

CHAPTER 5

CYCLE INTERRUPTED

I CAN'T LET HIM GO

This is a hard chapter to read. Loss of control is the greatest challenge a woman will ever face. I love women. I love the freedom in a woman's expression, the glory of her sexual step in the park. Her heel's arch speaks of courage to stand out in a fragile and precarious world. A woman can walk, talk, dance, sing, or cry anywhere and it's accepted. Loss of this expression's power and voice are a tragedy. In a relationship, damage is inevitable but some events and actions result in a crippling result. I am going to discuss some relationship triggers that create an inability for a woman to cycle out of a failed relationship into a healthy new one. In some cases, these acts of terror cause a woman to feel like she can't leave a toxic situation at all.

Eminem and Rihanna have a duet they perform, that makes women cry and shake their head at the same time. It's called **"Love the Way You Lie."** Anyone who's heard it knows what I mean.

Most women have lived it or know a woman who has. The abuse, control, and tragedy that the song denotes really strike a chord with women specifically. How hard is it to love a man who's not right for you? How hard is it to cover the physical scars you've received from the gift of his anger's punch with the foundation of your denial's blush? When you cry out only you hear because your voice's value has been silenced from long ago, by your loving father's cruel and un-affirming judgments. The sense of yourself that abides within your damaged hearts center, always seems to pour out in a negative and unsettling tone. Loving yourself isn't practical or efficient. When a woman put's her highest aspiration in the hands of a man's capable and controlling hands, she's in for the wrong kind of adventure. Let's add some clarity to how this bullshit plays out.

You're a blonde and always have been. Never an issue that elicited any response from men but praise and appreciation from in the past. Ben likes women with dark hair, boobs for days, minus ass for years. Did I mention the dark hair needs to be butt-length? Did I mention every other inch of your body needs to be hair-less?

He has a picture in his head that his woman needs to match. When you both met he was so taken by you he forgot himself for a moment. Only a moment though because women are on turbo when it comes to commitment. The purpose of taking your time is to weed out controlling assholes but after two weeks this stud was already your man so no worries. Men like this know they only need a moment.

Ben got you to die your hair black and now you look like you practice Wiccan. You have boobs but they aren't as perky as they could be, well according to Ben they aren't. For him, only DDD's are perky, everything else looks deflated. No worries, you got that situation handled. You had always thought about it so the nine thousand dollars you saved up to go to culinary school was the perfect down payment towards the 20 thousand needed for mega boobs. Now let's talk about the porn level ass you have going on under your Apple Bottom jeans.

Your waist is only 25 inches around, stomach washboard. Your hips are a solid 38 inches of "Baby got back!" level heaven. Ass for days but certainly not years. Ben is like, "It gets in the way baby…I want to feel more of you". Hmmm…maybe some lipo? Ben's happy with that scenario. I mean, nothing can be done about your personality as it is abstract so we'll stop there as I think the point has been made. After all this work Ben becomes insecure because his investment is being seen by other men.

Now he texts every day because his investment's location must be known. No going out with the girlfriends past midnight, and no girl trips of any kind. You got more attention as a blonde but Ben's freaking out because his ideal is walking around unattended. He's infatuated with a fantasy he wants to control but can't. His job is to make you feel like he can with tactics that come out of the oldest handbook of all time. It's a bitch-tracking algorithm called "Where the fuck are you, who with, and for what purpose?" You call it misery. This algorithm requires your identity to be under the sole control and influence of Ben only, therefore all outside influences must be suppressed.

Now you want to break free but you can't because who you are is locked up in Ben's defined bullshit realm of your existence. You're too embarrassed to admit that he has this much control. Catfights ensue with your girlfriends over this guy's influence over every decision you make. They are offering to die your hair black blonde, and you're not having it because your investment in this lie is too deep, and your relationship judgment and credibility is on the line. All this changes when you catch Ben fucking a dark haired Latina in the bedroom of your shared condo. She's everything you paid good money to be. He claims that it's a one-time mistake and tells you that you're taking it to hard. Now he's shaping the way you are supposed to respond to disrespect and disregard. You forgive him and change your hair color from subtle black to "Raven". Let's stop right here because I don't know who you are at this point and I'm writing about you.

Your name is Grace and you're a blonde. Your boobs are a 36D, we already know how delicious the rest is. Now you're a 38 F and your hair is Raven black. When I see your piercing blue eyes I think, "This bitch is going to eat my soul!" Just leave Ben and be happy. But the issue is who are you going to be happy with? Who are you? Without a base identity there's no way to cycle out of a relationship. You never formed a collective relationship identity with Ben, just changed who you were to please his sensibility and taste. And to maintain this new identity you need constant feedback from him because his judgment and instruction is the key to your reality, nothing else feels safe... including being yourself. You decided you weren't good enough so why trust you now. This state of mind requires an intervention. This has to be physical first, mental second.

Change your hair back to its natural color. Not a different color, as close to the natural hue as possible. If you had bush down there before, let it grow back. If you used to tweeze, tweeze again. You have to remind your mental self of who the real you is again. Only then will mental realignment occur. Your mind will now re-associate your original habits and behaviors back with the real you it recognizes. Now begin to appreciate those habits on a deeper and more defined level. Keep the boobs, just keep them. Yes I'm a boob man. Yes, I want them as big as they can be. I'm telling you from a total biased opinion and place of consciousness, and I'm right on the money here. Just keep them. Dramatic medical procedures require thought and judgment when initiated, even more if and when reversed. You're going to be angry that you succumbed to the controlling nature of this man to this extent. Never go into an important decision in life in the state of anger. Anger is a state that you need to be in for reflection, not action. When anger is acted upon hastily damage is always the result. Your frame can handle the breast size. Wait until they wear out in 10 years and then make an informed and researched decision based on how you feel at that time. Who knows, you might grow to like them. I'm pulling for that outcome. On to the next scenario.

Phillip is your knight in shining armor. He opens doors. He walks on the street side of the sidewalk. The word beautiful has no power because he uses it so much in describing your person. Your friends think he's a movie star that for some reason settled for a skank like you. You love this...nothing better than having your dearest and closest friends jealous of you to the point of hate and discontent! The value felt by you can't be underestimated. You weren't keen on yourself before you met him. His value gives

yours meaning and heft. His money gives your poverty

irrelevance. You're not broke but compared to his capacity... You

get the point?

Tonight's dinner is going to be special. Lasagna, his favorite.

You serve him in lingerie, and kiss the back of his ear. He takes

one look at you and says, "Why so slutty tonight?" This is the first

time you've ever done this for him or any man for that matter and

you're feeling very vulnerable. You want to be his fantasy so you

play along with the fantasy. "I'm your slut tonight baby, and any

other night you want me to be". He says, "I don't" and tells you to

stop tramping around like a thirsty bitch and to put your clothes

back on. Something snapped in him and you're alarmed, really

hurt by his change in tone and intention. You lash out verbally in

defense of your loving action and he straight slaps you and says,

"Don't ever rise up or raise your voice against me again!!!" Now

you're scared, and you don't what comes next. Your heartbeat

raises in intensity and pace. A cold sweat startles your cheeks

sensation. All you hear inside is, "Get the fuck out of here now!!!" You apologize to Phillip and go change. You tell him you forgot the parmesan cheese in the car and you walk out the front door calmly to get it. You run at full speed. The car is your savior right now. He peaks through the window and sees you running and takes off after you. He looks sorry, his body language says come back because I love you. You drive off like you're at the Pomona speedway. You call the police, file a complaint, have him arrested, and go about your normal life after the restraining order's filed. You tell your two brother's what happened and they pay Phillip a visit. They say, "Hit, touch, talk to, or call our sister again and you're dead, fucking dead!"

No, that's not what happened. You didn't run off because after he hit you he immediately apologized and said his anger got the best of him. He said it would never happen again. Same physical response from you though; rapid heartbeat, cold sweat, and an undeniable urge to get the fuck out. It's called the fight or flight response and you ignored its purpose.

Its purpose is to get you to safety. Every cell in your body is heightened to this purpose. You have extra strength, heightened mental acuity, and increased stamina and endurance. You use none of it. You ignore the impulse and stay in the danger zone. He didn't kill you, just slapped you. You don't realize that you just turned off your body's impulse to save itself and you might not be able to turn it back on in connection with this man's destructive and violent energy.

I was trying to get a client to submit to the Relationship Recovery Cycle. She expressed to me that even though she had been free of her ex-boyfriend's grasp for months she always felt like she couldn't leave him totally. He always had this weird emotional access to her that she couldn't break. It wasn't her soul because she knew he would never be a mate to that aspect who she was. She couldn't break his conscious grip on her mind or say she would never physically see him again. I then intuitively said something to her that I had never heard before. And it changed her life.

"You're addicted to him....just like a drug. You're an addict and your addiction is to your ex boyfriends physical and mental abuse. The physical component and your response to it specifically, is the catalyst. It opens the doorway to the mental control aspect."

When the fight or flight response comes and you ignore its call to flee, but instead go right back into the presence of its catalyst, a chemical reaction is set off in the body, just like with cocaine, opium or meth. The first time you indulge in these pursuits should always be your last. When you engage in them your body first says, "Never again" and gives physical cues to reinforce this truth. The greatest example would be with alcohol. This is a nuanced example but the closest in mirroring the effect I'm talking about. Everyone acknowledges that drinking in moderation can be a blast. It releases inhibition and causes your internal self to express freely. Drinking to alcohol poison levels however, can set off a chemical chain of events in your body that you can't come back from. If after experiencing this level of intoxication you go back and do it again, you'll find yourself addicted to a state of being that can at best hamper every aspect of your life's expression...at worst kill you.

Moderation represents rough sex, an intense physical connection

with another soul. A slap in the name of love is not a slap at all, but

a slap in response to love from a place of hate is to be avoided at all

costs. I realize every woman doesn't want to be slapped during sex

but for those in the know, slapping face and ass during intimacy can

take you to a different dimension. There's pleasure in moderation

even in the context of pain. When pain received is a statement of

implied worthlessness and a precursor for oppressive control…that's

a poison you don't want to be addicted to.

My client expressed how during one particular night of arguing

that her then man got violent and threw something across the room.

When she tried to leave he dragged her by her feet back into the

bedroom. Not hit, but still violence. She went back to him, forgave

him and now she can't let go. A person that has an addiction can't

cycle out of it, he or she has to leave it and never return to it.

I explained that the Relationship Recovery Cycle didn't apply in

this case. She was an addict and he was her drug, that's how she

should see it. I then said you have to leave him. Just leave and don't look back. An alcoholic first has to acknowledge that he will always be an alcoholic, that's how AA works. He first states his name then says he's addicted to alcohol. For an addict's acknowledgment leads to freedom, not a cycle. He or she has most likely been in denial for a good part of the disease's manifestation, so this is critical. After you acknowledge this you just don't drink. You don't go to where alcohol is easily accessible or available at all. You just stay away. A substance has you, but you don't live in that reality. You make a conscious decision to avoid its reach. My client needed to stay away from her ex-boyfriend. She needed to not engage in any form of communication or exchange with this man. Once the physical addiction is established the mental control and reinforcement of its power continues.

What if you have a child or children with this man? The rule still applies. This is physical, that's the missing component in a lot of people's theories about abuse even though it's initiated physically. A woman can physically be addicted to being hit by a man she has yielded that authority to. My client was set free through the awareness I am sharing right now. I realize I'm not a doctor and don't have the legal right to assert my opinions or views as an actual medical diagnosis. I have a theory. I'm sharing it. It's not a dangerous theory. It's not earth-shattering and in no way encourages deviant behavior, unsafe actions, or belief in an unfounded philosophy. We all agree that physical and mental abuse is not conducive to a loving soul's health, vitality or happiness. We all agree that the best action by a woman being physically assaulted is to get away from the source of that abuse to a place of safety. My theory is that so many women are stuck in a physically abusive relationship due to their initial response to the violent act. They acted in opposition to their body's fight or flight response, which sets off a chemical release that supports the body's survival mechanism. The purpose of this release is to supply the body with every natural resource physiologically necessary for fleeing from the source of the danger present, in this case the abusive male. When a woman consciously makes a decision to ignore her survival imperative she creates an addictive dynamic between her and her abuser.

My advice is simple. You have a one hundred percent chance of not experiencing this addiction pattern in any intimate relationship by severing it at the first act of physical abuse. I would not advise a woman to continue any form of relationship with a man that exhibits this type of behavior. He is clearly showing a lack of understanding and sensitivity. He should modify his behavior in order to experience relationship success and universal harmony in life in general.

My dad used to say there's nothing more important in your life than your name Tony. People can take your money, fame, power, and physical possessions but your good name endures. I believed him not because it's a true statement. That is up for debate. I believed him because he was my dad. I believed everything my dad said. A daughter believes in her father even more, if that were possible. How a father sees his daughter helps to shape who she is. Sometimes this is a good thing, sometimes not so good. It's our job as parent's to see and articulate the nature of each of our children, not program them into the image of who we want them to be. Let's look at how a father's reflection in a daughter's behavior affects her relationship and causes her not to cycle into or out of any relationship.

Sheryl is a guy's girl. She love's sports, drinks beer and revels in the occasional freedom fuck. No strings attached, just reckless abandon via her glory hole. Relationships are obstructions to her expressions movement. Some women have a healthy understanding of a relationship's timing, no rush is ever needed. Sheryl however has never been relationship minded which irks the men she dates. She's a guy's dream at first as he feels no pressure to invest or really connect at first. There's no pretense of ownership and for the beginning phase this suits him just fine. But as he begins to be enamored by Sheryl's sense of play and grasp of everything guy he notices a few things that make his eyebrow raise.

Sheryl has no sense of ownership at all. When she's out with a guy no one can tell because she's not a hand holder or even an eye-contact catcher. She smiles like it's her mission in life to do so and every guy feels her heat. If you grab Sheryl's ass she's probably going to grab back, stranger or not. She's not giving her number away; she knows who she's with. She's just not sweating it but her dude is, trust. Sheryl takes days to return a text. She dresses up nice, but your three inches taller than she is before the six inch heels...she's five foot nine by the way. Then she brings up the height difference to make you feel like a dwarf. Her guy's getting fucked that night so should he care?

Sheryl was raised by a father who wanted a son. He put her in sports from the age of five, and pushed her like she had a set of iron balls. He loved her deeply but her persona never matched his dream or aspiration. Sheryl felt this and became one of the guys to receive that love. Now everyone she dates feels the wrath of that love. She wants the same thing every other woman wants, connection. Her way to connection isn't a way at all however...she's kind of a train wreck relationally. No need to cycle out of a relationship that never developed into one in the first place. How she received her identity and sense of self as a child affected her relational capacity.

You might be thinking what does this have to do with the statement under the chapter heading, "I can't let him go". It matters because Sheryl can't let go of her father's affirmation of who she is.

He's dead now and her reference point for receiving love from a man is to be one of the guys. Now she needs to get a new vision for who she is in reality. How is this done?

It's done through love and patience. Sheryl needs to cycle out of the first and most important opposite sex relationship in her life, the one with her father. Under normal circumstances this asexual relationship runs its course in a natural and fluid manner. First her dad is her hero, then her friend, then her enemy, then this old guy that's out of touch with every important connection she has to reality. At this point she's ready to fill that empty space with a new, un-informed idiot that has the wisdom of a shelled peanut. He's called your first love ladies and as a father he is universally hated by us. Even if we act like we love him we don't. We hate him. He's a stupid ass chipmunk with a dick that never sleeps and his only goal is to fuck you into a confused coma of impossible dreams and poverty. I'm a little biased…you think

Sheryl didn't experience this separation into idiot-heaven because her father was being treated for pancreatic cancer while she was in college and she still loved him to death despite having the nickname

Shark. Yeah, he wanted a son. His last words before he went were,

"I love you Shark, don't let these rat bastard, fucktards get the best

of you, I taught you better than that". Sheryl cried and said goodbye

to her father. Now when Sheryl meets a guy he's a fucktard until

proven otherwise. She has no trust in engaging in men because the

one man she loved made her a guy and why let a low-life fucktard

make her a girl. Sex for her is about power and maintaining control,

not connection with another loving being.

Define yourself according to the divine prerogative within your

soul's identity. Never let someone corner you into a classification

that stifles your creative expression. Forgive your father, or mother,

or brother, or older sister, or whoever made you into something you

aren't. Then forgive yourself for buying into it. Sheryl's beautiful

by the way, just like every other woman who walks this amazing

planet.

Treat everyone's heart like the heart of a child. Treat everyone's

soul like the pedal of a rose, treat everyone's shit like shit, and stay

out of its odor's reach

Anthony Brown-2015

CHAPTER 6

DON'T SKIP PHASES IN THE CYCLE!

WHATEVER YOU SKIP YOU AMPLIFY

A micro chapter on this subject to clarify something. I thought about adding this to chapter 5 because it is a cycle interruption but decided it deserved its own separate space and context. Skipping a phase in the cycle has a consequence. Let's discuss it briefly.

I was talking to a female client and she expressed excitement about giving the cycle process a try. She was stuck emotionally in an unhealthy dynamic with her ex-boyfriend and wanted a change of consciousness and attitude regarding it. When she got to the end of sadness she expressed difficulty with anger. She said she had never experienced anger in any recovery from a relationship before. She had skipped it. Her anger, however, was showing itself in an amplified manner in other areas of her life. I explained that when you skip a phase it amplifies the emotional state associated with it in other trigger areas until it's faced and released. Things that normally would make her a little angry would really set her off as long as she was in this state. I helped her get angry by speaking to her from a reference point of the anger sentiment that is common in this phase. She got angry, real angry. Now she is fully cycled out of that old relationship and enjoying her current single status to the fullest.

I recently had an impromptu session with a woman that a friend referred me to. She said her friend was having a relationship issue so I listened. She expressed how she had been in a relationship of almost 2 years and that she was really having a hard time letting go. She began to cry shortly after she expounded on it. She expressed how she had been in a physically abusive relationship in the past but had cut off all ties and communication with the man. I knew that wasn't the issue because she took the correct course of action per my theory. She then started talking about events that took place farther back and expressed that she had been date raped. I could see in her change of emotional state that it caused an issue. As she spoke of it she stopped crying and became numb. We had established that she had an amplified expression of sadness prior to this but now I knew the root. She turned off a certain part of her emotional being after she had gotten raped to cope in the aftermath. Now, because she wasn't emotionally whole inside, she couldn't and had no willingness to fully engage in the sadness phase of the Relationship Recovery Cycle. She acknowledged that she had always skipped that aspect of her recovery in all her relationships up to this point. This started after she experienced that horrifying and violently abusive act. I knew this had to be addressed so I walked her through the steps in a clearing exercise on the spot and dispersed the block that was causing her not to process sadness appropriately. It was a life-changing experience for her, me as well. She now had the full presence of emotional consciousness needed to engage in the sadness phase of the recovery cycle and renew and refresh her soul, mind and body to be ready for new love.

My processes, techniques, and wisdom have full effectivity when followed in their entirety. Skipping or rushing through phases in the cycle have consequences. My desire is for you to have a transformational and impactful experience in walking through these natural processes. My ultimate aspiration is your loving expression being amplified, not just for the sake of a healthy relationship, but in life wholly.

Whatever process you skip over in life doesn't get to receive the

benefit of your transformational footprint's impression...every

experience deserves your beauty's shadow

Anthony Brown – 2016

CHAPTER 7

SOUL TIES

I COULD WRITE A WHOLE BOOK ABOUT THIS CHAPTER'S SUBJECT

One of the most significant factors that I have seen in Relationship Recovery Cycle issues with my clients is soul ties.

I'm going to challenge people's beliefs here but it needs to be done. The concept I share is universally understood and anyone reading this male or female can relate no matter what level of buy in you give to the philosophy behind this. I will start by defining a soul tie from my perspective and just dive in.

Soul Tie – An immediate connection you have with another human being that is not

predicated upon time, space, proximity or development of traditional awareness or physical

chemistry.

You meet someone. Immediately you feel a chemistry and connection that isn't based on the amount of time you've known them, awareness you currently have of them, or even any overwhelming physical attraction. The point is you know this person and you don't know how or why. Conversations feel like you're catching up on old times more than getting to know them afresh. When they touch you it's not about butterflies, you've felt like you needed their touch your whole life. You want this person immediately and they're not even your type. Things he does that would drive you crazy from another guy, you give him a pass on and you do it easily. Or the opposite, you get angry and reactive in response to things he does that never would normally bother you in another man. The key is you feel a tie to this being's soul that you can't and don't want to break. You're with him from the moment you meet, Skype, Facetime, or sometimes even hear his voice in a verbal exchange. Your souls are tied together from past experience even though you just met.

I believe these are from actual past live experiences but anyone can at least admit that you feel like you have legitimate history with this person. When you are intimate with a person and this dynamic is present it's not new, it just feels like an extension of you breathing. The nervousness of the first time is almost never present. What the hell are you going to do about this?

If you've found your soulmate than go for it. If they feel the same it's a reunion of sorts. The issue is the current situation and circumstance almost never matches the past experiences dynamic. How many women have met this man when they were already married? How many men are irked by this connectivity because the relational history may have an abuse component that isn't relatable in the present. What I'm actually saying is just as strange as it's implied to be. I have met women that treated me like I was abusive or harsh when I wasn't. They might have described abusive situations in the past with other men and the behavior I'm displaying is nowhere near that but they are still viscerally taking it that way or worse. I get that the past pain from the old relationship might be triggering a reaction but what I'm implying is that some past-life negative experience with me that needs to be atoned for is actually to blame. I know that's far out but I actually have experienced this. The key in all of this is no matter what you might believe, for some reason you honestly feel like you know this man, are aware of parts of his nature that you couldn't know without past history with him, and believe you belong to and with him. It's not rational in the present sense but very powerful none the less….so what do you do?

You accept it and let it be. Sounds easy but it's not. You have to release from control of outcome in this case. You have to let it be, to flow through you. You might be with someone else at the time. I'm not saying leave a current relationship to respond to this connection, just saying let it be. Let it be as in process how you feel about it and acknowledge that it's in the past. Even if you just met him the connectivity isn't based on present conditions or circumstances. If you have a strong sexual attraction to this man and you're in a current relationship honor your current relationship. You might think "We're meant to be together" but the truth is you already were. You don't have to believe this literally but it's honestly how you'll feel. How can a woman want to fuck a man she doesn't presently know or have any traditional awareness, safety and sexual chemistry established with over her current man that's she's known for a year that she has verifiable, dynamic and enjoyable connectivity with? This is a clear sign of a soul tie being present.

Soul ties are usually best broken or released with both party's agreement. It would be easy if one party could do it. The easiest thing is to keep a clear head and be present. If this guy is in Paris, France and you're in New York and you're engaged to a great guy that is present and in your physical proximity then get married and just keep a place in your heart for Paris. You won't cycle out of love with Paris...your connection with him is not based on present reality but a past one. That's how you have to see it. You haven't been in any kind of present relationship to justify how you feel. You met this guy on a business trip and had to talk with him. You smelled his scent and wanted to sleep with him. When you left Paris you missed him more than your fiancée and you just met the guy. You didn't sleep with him but you're acting like you've slept with him for years. Trust me when I say this happens to women.

If you actually have the opportunity to get into an active relationship with a man that you already have an established soul tie with then understand that if you break up the recovery cycle will be amplified at the very least and at the most ineffective. Luckily this doesn't happen often but when it does either you both release each other consciously or you live with the connection and manage your life with it as a component of your emotional being.

Let's say you believed me for a moment to my fullest degree and you were married to this guy in a past life for 50 years. Let's say you lost him tragically and never got over it in the lifetime in question. You meet up with him again in this life and you have 50 years of past life history with this man and you've known your boyfriend for 6 months. Your current boyfriend doesn't stand a chance in an emotional attachment sense. What if you were part of an indigenous tribe and this man swept you up in a raid and married you by force? When you relate to him there are certain things he does that instill a fear and insecurity in you that's not normal for you. What if you grew to love him? So you have this push and pull of fear and attachment going on with this guy that you don't understand. You've dated men in the past that you wouldn't give the time of day if you felt unsafe for a minute but this guy can scare you half to death and somehow you're still okay with it.

The present situation you are living in and your current destiny have a lot to do with the place a soul tie should have in your life. If his goals, vision and direction don't align with yours then it's best to leave the feelings you have at the processing stage and not act them out with him. It takes a lot of strength to resist getting entangled in a connection that although so strong will only lead you off your path. Every woman has this strength inherently within them. With everything a woman faces in relationship recovery it would have been disingenuous for me not to tackle this issue.

If you have ever had, are actively in, or will sometime in the future face the dynamics of a soul tie follow these 3 rules:

1. *If you are in a fulfilling relationship when this occurs don't leave it*

2. *Soul ties are broken with agreement from both parties*

3. *This relationship and connection is based on a past reality, not a present one*

I have really enjoyed sharing this. I feel great freedom from helping others reach their highest potential in a relationship. Meeting, relating and growing in love with another soul is so fulfilling. We are beings made up of love. We package it in the being of who we are and share it from the heart of our purpose's reach. Never forget that change is inevitable but our response to it is always our personal choice to make. Everyone reading this book is loved and appreciated by me...one love.

I know

I see

I believe

I am

The manifestation

Of love's cry

Crying out

To humanity

For help

For love's imperative

Needs the help of all…its beautiful citizens

Seeing you here

In my life's vision

Makes me happy

Read my heart's prerogative

Share in the warmth of its message…

of peace

Stay connected to you

Because in you is me

And in me is her

And in her is him

And in him is them

One love for all to be fed from

Driven by

And held accountable to

I wish everyone reading this book a peace and clarity

That speaks of their birth's power and resonance

Anthony Brown-2015

www.ingramcontent.com/pod-product-compliance
Lightning Source LLC
Chambersburg PA
CBHW030154070426
42447CB00032B/1195